Autho

This book features 100 influential and inspiring quotes by Marilyn Monroe. Undoubtedly, this collection will give you a huge boost of inspiration.

1

"I'm selfish, impatient and a little insecure. I make mistakes, I am out of control and at times hard to handle. But if you can't handle me at my worst, then you sure as hell don't deserve me at my best."

2

"I believe that everything happens for a reason. People change so that you can learn to let go, things go wrong so that you appreciate them when they're right, you believe lies so you eventually learn to trust no one but yourself, and sometimes good things fall apart so better things can fall together."

3

"Imperfection is beauty, madness is genius and it's better to be absolutely ridiculous than absolutely boring."

4

"If you can make a woman laugh,
you can make her do anything."

5

"The real lover is the man who can thrill you by kissing your forehead or smiling into your eyes or just staring into space."

6

"A wise girl kisses but doesn't love, listens but doesn't believe, and leaves before she is left."

7

"I am good, but not an angel. I do sin, but I am not the devil. I am just a small girl in a big world trying to find someone to love."

8

"If you're gonna be two-faced at least make one of them pretty."

9

"It's far better to be unhappy alone than unhappy with someone — so far."

10

"When it comes down to it, I let them think what they want. If they care enough to bother with what I do, then I'm already better than them."

11

"I've never fooled anyone. I've let people fool themselves. They didn't bother to find out who and what I was. Instead they would invent a character for me. I wouldn't argue with them. They were obviously loving somebody I wasn't."

12

"We should all start to live before we get too old. Fear is stupid. So are regrets."

13

"She was a girl who knew how to be happy even when she was sad. And that's important—you know."

14

"All little girls should be told they are pretty, even if they aren't."

15

"It's not true that I had nothing on. I had the radio on."

16

"Beneath the makeup and behind the smile I am just a girl who wishes for the world."

17

"I don't mind living in a man's world, as long as I can be a woman in it."

18

"The nicest thing for me is sleep,
then at least I can dream."

19

"Who said nights were for sleep?"

20

"You believe lies so you eventually learn to trust no one but yourself."

21

"All we demanded was our right to twinkle."

22

"It's often just enough to be with someone. I don't need to touch them. Not even talk. A feeling passes between you both. You're not alone."

23

"Dogs never bite me. Just humans."

24

"If I'd observed all the rules I'd never have got anywhere."

25

"Keep smiling, because life is a beautiful thing and there's so much to smile about."

26

"Success makes so many people hate you. I wish it wasn't that way. It would be wonderful to enjoy success without seeing envy in the eyes of those around you."

27

"I want to grow old without facelifts. I want to have the courage to be loyal to the face I have made."

28

"Sometimes things fall apart so that better things can fall together."

29

"I don't know who invented high heels, but all women owe him a lot!"

30

"Wanting to be someone else is a waste of the person you are."

31

"All a girl really wants is for one guy to prove to her that they are not all the same."

32

"I don't mind making jokes, but I don't want to look like one."

33

"Sex is part of nature. I go along with nature."

34

"You never know what life is like, until you have lived it."

35

"We are all born sexual creatures, thank God, but it's a pity so many people despise and crush this natural gift."

36

"I restore myself when I'm alone."

37

"I just want to be wonderful."

38

"It's all make believe, isn't it?"

"Boys think girls are like books,
If the cover doesn't catch their
eye they won't bother to read
what's inside."

40

"I don't mind being burdened with being glamorous and sexual. Beauty and femininity are ageless and can't be contrived, and glamour, although the manufacturers won't like this, cannot be manufactured. Not real glamour; it's based on femininity."

41

"The body is meant to be seen,
not all covered up."

42

"I have feelings too. I am still human. All I want is to be loved, for myself and for my talent. "

43

"I'm not interested in money, I just want to be wonderful."

44

"What do I wear in bed? Well, Chanel No. 5, of course"

45

"I'm very definitely a woman
and I enjoy it. "

46

"Hollywood is a place where they'll pay you a thousand dollars for a kiss and fifty cents for your soul. I know, because I turned down the first offer often enough and held out for the fifty cents."

47

"I used to think as I looked out on the Hollywood night — there must be thousands of girls sitting alone like me, dreaming of becoming a movie star. But I'm not going to worry about them. I'm dreaming the hardest."

48

"If I play a stupid girl and ask a stupid question, I've got to follow it through, what am I supposed to do, look intelligent?"

49

"Before marriage, a girl has to make love to a man to hold him. After marriage, she has to hold him to make love to him."

50

"Just because you fail once doesn't mean you're gonna fail at everything."

51

"I've been on a calendar, but never on time."

52

"I live to suceed, not to please you or anyone else."

53

"To all the girls that think you're fat because you're not a size zero, you're the beautiful one, its society who's ugly."

54

"This life is what you make it. Not matter what, you're going to mess up sometimes, it's a universal truth. But the good part is you get to decide how you're going to mess it up. Girls will be your friends – they'll act like it anyway. But just remember, some come, somg go. The ones that stay with you through everything – they're your true best friends. Don't let go of them."

55

"Too often they don't realize
what they have until it's gone.
They're too stubborn to say,
'Sorry, I was wrong'
they hurt the ones closest to
their hearts,
and we let the most foolish
things tear us apart."

56

"I love to do the things the censors won't pass."

57

"I have too many fantasies to be a housewife.... I guess I am a fantasy."

58

"I learned to walk as a baby and I haven't had a lesson since."

59

"How wrong it is for a woman to expect the man to build the world she wants, rather than to create it herself."

60

"Your clothes should be tight enough to show you're a woman but loose enough to show you're a lady."

61

"A career is wonderful, but you can't curl up with it on a cold night."

62

"A sex symbol becomes a thing. I hate being a thing."

63

"Just because you fall once, doesn't mean you're fall at everything. Keep trying, hold on, and always trust yourself, because if you don't then who will?"

64

"Dreaming about being an actress, is more exciting then being one."

65

"I knew I belonged to the public and to the world, not because I was talented or even beautiful, but because I had never belonged to anything or anyone else."

66

"Looking back, I guess I used to play-act all the time. For one thing, it meant I could live in a more interesting world than the one around me."

67

"I am invariably late for appointments - sometimes as much as two hours. I've tried to change my ways but the things that make me late are too strong, and too pleasing."

68

"Some people have been unkind.
If I say I want to grow as an
actress, they look at my figure.
If I say I want to develop, to
learn my craft, they laugh.
Somehow they don't expect me
to be serious about my work."

69

"It's better to be absolutely ridiculous than absolutely boring."

70

"When you're young and healthy you can plan on Monday to commit suicide, and by Wednesday you're laughing again."

71

"I read poetry to save time."

72

"I could never pretend
something I didn't feel. I could
never make love if I didn't love,
and if I loved I could no more
hide the fact than change the
color of my eyes."

73

"A girl doesn't need anyone who
doesn't need her."

74

"I'm for the individual as opposed to the corporation. The way it is the individual is the underdog, and with all the things a corporation has going for them the individual comes out banged on her head. The artist is nothing. It's really tragic. "

75

"I've often stood silent at a party for hours listening to my movie idols turn into dull and little people. "

76

"The thing I want more than anything else? I want to have children. I used to feel for every child I had, I would adopt another."

77

"That's the way you feel when you're beaten inside. You don't feel angry at those who've beaten you. You just feel ashamed."

78

"A wise girl knows her limits, a smart girl knows that she has none."

79

"No one ever told me I was pretty when I was a little girl. All little girls should be told they're pretty, even if they aren't."

80

"So keep your head high, keep your chin up, and most importantly, keep smiling, because life's a beautiful thing and there's so much to smile about."

81

"I don't stop when I'm tired. I only stop when I'm done ..."

82

"I want to grow old without facelifts... I want to have the courage to be loyal to the face I've made. Sometimes I think it would be easier to avoid old age, to die young, but then you'd never complete your life, would you? You'd never wholly know you."

83

"Husbands are chiefly good as lovers when they are betraying their wives."

84

"The trouble with censors is that
they worry if a girl has cleavage.
They ought to worry if she
hasn't any."

85

"Suicide, is a persons privilege. I don't believe it's a sin or a crime it's your right if you do. Though it doesn't get you anywhere."

86

"Men are always ready to respect
anything that bores them."

87

"For those who are poor in happiness, each time is a first time; happiness never becomes a habit."

88

"A strong man doesn't have to be
dominant toward a woman. He
doesn't match his strength
against a woman weak with love
for him. He matches it against
the world."

89

"You might as well make yourself fly as to make yourself love."

90

"There's only one sort of natural blonde on earth - albinos."

91

"Always, always, always believe in yourself, because if you don't, then who will, Sweetie? So keep your head high, keep your chin up, and most importantly, keep smiling, because life's a beautiful thing and there's so much to smile about."

"I would have told her then she was the only thing that I could love in this dying world but the simple word "love" itself already died and went away."

"It's better for the whole world
to know you, even as a sex star,
than never to be known at all."

"Trying to build myself up with the fact that I have done things right that were even good and have had moments that were excellent but the bad is heavier to carry around and feel have no confidence."

95

"I wanted to ask a thousand questions, but there was no one to ask. Besides I knew that people only told lies to children—lies about everything from soup to Santa Claus."

"People had a habit of looking at me as if I were some kind of mirror instead of a person. They didn't see me, they saw their own lewd thoughts, then they white-masked themselves by calling me the lewd one."

"Imperfection is beauty,
madness is genius."

"But chiefly, no lies! No lies about there being a Santa Claus or about the world being full of noble and honorable people all eager to help each other and do good to each other. I'll tell her there are honor and goodness in the world, the same as there are diamonds and radium."

99

"They will only care when you're gone."

100

"I am not a victim of emotional conflicts. I am human."

Made in the USA
Las Vegas, NV
22 December 2023

83435228R00056